The Catholic Survival Guide to Dating & Relationships

by
Mary Beth Bonacci

*All booklets are published thanks to the
generous support of the members of the
Catholic Truth Society*

CATHOLIC TRUTH SOCIETY

PUBLISHERS TO THE HOLY SEE

Contents

Images: Composite visuals In-house CTS.

Original edition *Real Love* © Copyright 2012 Ignatius Press, San Francisco.

ISBN 978 1 78469 132 5

Introduction

When I was at university, I attended a lecture series on a subject that, at the time, had not been receiving much attention on university campuses – or anywhere else. That subject was chastity.

Up to that time, I had always been a "nice Catholic girl". I knew the Church forbade premarital sex, and I had complied. I had even become fairly adept at the "I'm not that kind of girl" speech. But I wasn't exactly sure why. I knew it had something to do with not getting pregnant and not going to hell. (You're a nice boy, and I'm sure sex is fun if you say it is. But forever is a very long time, and I don't want to spend it in a climate quite so warm.) Of course, these aren't bad reasons to abstain, but neither do they give the whole story.

Like every unmarried Christian, I had struggled with questions. How far is too far? How do I know when I am in love? How do I say no nicely? When should I break up with someone? How should I break up with someone? Why does the Church teach what she does? Like most people, I found far too few answers.

I had rarely even heard the word "chastity". I was familiar with the term "abstinence", and that was what I was practising. The problem with abstinence, of course, was that I didn't really see anything positive about it, aside from avoiding the more unpleasant realities of teen pregnancy and eternal damnation.

Thus, what I heard in my senior year in those chastity talks enthralled me. The word "chastity" brought my understanding of the gift of sexuality to a whole new level. This was not just about avoiding unpleasant consequences. This was a complete "owner's manual" for our bodies. This was about understanding, finding and living love.

Human sexuality is a gift – an incredible, beautiful, precious gift from God. I had certainly heard that in vague terms before, but no one had ever brought the reality home to me as did this series of talks. Like any gift, sexuality is designed for use in a certain context – in this case, in the context of a loving marriage. In that context, it is an incredible instrument of the transmission of God's own love and life. Outside of that context, it can be damaged, and it can cause damage. I certainly didn't have to look far to see that kind of damage. After that talk, I began to look around me and to assess what I had been seeing over the past years. I saw the damage right there in my own generation. But those who were abstaining seemed to be doing better – and not just in avoiding pregnancy and disease. Love was going better. Relationships were going better. They were more easily able to leave when things were not working out. There was less turmoil in their lives. They were happier.

I had discovered the difference between chastity and mere abstinence. Abstinence is negative. It is about what you don't do. Chastity is positive. It is a virtue. It is about understanding and living real love, not just in dating, but in every area of life.

Real love seeks not just to satisfy itself. In real love, we look out for what is best for the other. That is what chastity helps us to do – to understand the precious gift of sexuality, and to respect it in ourselves and others, so that we can really love each other instead of using each other. That kind of love – real, honest, self-giving love – is rare in this day and age.

At the time I realised all of this, I was working with pregnant teenagers at a pregnancy centre. I kept thinking, "If only I had talked to you two months ago." It was so clear to me that their sexual activity was fuelled by an unfulfilled desire for real love. I was tired of dealing with the consequences. I wanted to get to the root of the problem. Then I had another radical idea. "Why don't I go to schools and talk about chastity? Others are probably asking all the same questions I've asked. I would have loved to have had someone talk to me about all of this when I was a teenager." It seemed like a pretty novel idea at the time. I wasn't aware of anyone else speaking on the subject. (In fact, a handful of others around the country were getting the same novel idea at about the same time. Isn't it funny how God works?) Of course, I had no intention of making this kind of work a career. This was just supposed to be the good deed I did on Wednesday afternoons while I climbed the corporate ladder. I expected audiences to be interested, to be sure. I was convinced then, as I am now, that most people are attracted to chastity, even if they don't know it. I couldn't possibly have predicted, however, the degree of enthusiasm this work would generate.

From the beginning, the students gave standing ovations. They kept me after the talks. They asked questions through their lunch breaks and long past school hours. The talks moved from classrooms to auditoriums to stadiums to TV studios; from high schools to university campuses to young adult and parent groups. My first post-university job quickly went by the wayside, and I dedicated myself to this work on a full-time basis. In all the years since, the work has continued to grow. The harvest is plenty. People of all ages are starved of this message, starved of guidance and starved of love. They are also starved of straight answers. One of my favourite parts of any presentation is the question and answer period. I always ask audiences to submit anonymous questions in writing, so that they feel free to ask any question without being identified.

Over the years, I've been asked a lot of questions. The questions I hear are often wonderful and insightful. Many are very personal. Far too many reflect long unaddressed pain. Many are the same questions I have asked and sometimes still ask. Audiences of all ages, in all areas of the country and in all the other countries I have visited ask the same questions. We all seem to struggle with the same problems and challenges. I have written this book to answer those questions. Every question you will find in these pages has actually been asked of me. These questions are representative of those I am most frequently asked. Most are taken directly from anonymous questions submitted in the context of a talk. Some are paraphrased from verbal questions asked after a talk. A few are from letters I have received. I have summarised these letters, changing any information that might identify their source, and included them here.

Many of these questions are from teenagers. As a single person well past my teens, however, I know that the answers apply not just to those under twenty, but to anyone who believes it is important to respect God's gift of sexuality while dating. It is a particular joy for me to work with other single people, knowing that we face the same struggles and challenges. I have always known that those of us who are unmarried need more than exhortations to abstinence. We need concrete help. We need to date well, so that we can marry well. We need to know how to take chastity from the realm of the conceptual to the realm of our everyday lives. We need divine support and, through him, the support of other single Christians. We need to know that others out there are on the same road we are. This book is my attempt to address those needs.

This work is not mine. It is God's, from end to end. I didn't invent chastity – he did. But I stand in awe of his incredible plan for love, and I enjoy nothing more than sharing it with any audience I can find. It is a blessing and an amazing privilege to be chosen to participate in his work in this way. There is an amazing hunger for love in today's world, and I honestly believe that chastity is the answer – his answer.

Chastity is love – real love.

PREPARING YOURSELF
for Love

"Why is chastity so important and what does it have to do with finding love?"

Chastity is important for a lot of reasons. It is important because it protects our relationships – with God and with each other. It is important because it helps us to find and to live real love. I honestly believe that chastity is the only way to find love in this love-starved world of ours.

Sexual attraction, at its most basic level, is a human drive, much like hunger or anger. Human drives, by themselves, don't know real love. Drives know only "I want what I want when I want it". When you are very hungry and you see a pizza, your drive wants to reach out, grab that pizza and eat it. It is your brain that says, "We are in a restaurant, and that pizza is on someone else's table. Also, the particular slice you are ogling happens to belong to a small child. Don't take it."

Taking the pizza would not be a loving thing, but your drive alone doesn't know that. Your brain has to be the one to break the news. Your brain cannot be very effective, however, if the drive doesn't listen. Your brain and your willpower must be stronger than your drives. This applies to many different situations. If you are angry, your anger drive may cause you to want to hit someone. It is your brain that says, "That is not loving." And when your sex drive says, "Sex would sure be fun right now", it is your brain that has to say no. It is our brains and our wills that choose to love, not our drives.

Chastity is about developing self-control. It means putting our drives under the control of our brains. Chastity means being able to say no when our drives are screaming "Yes!!!" Chastity helps us to find love in another way. It keeps our brains clear so that we can recognise the right person and get rid of the wrong people.

"Dating chaste" means spending your time doing positive, non-sexual things with this person. It means getting to know this person, spending your time together talking and having fun. It means seeing how this person reacts in different situations and how compatible the two of you are.

Chastity means not allowing the emotional bond that sex brings. It means allowing yourself to think clearly. Chastity doesn't mean that you are not sexually attracted to this person. It just means that you are controlling that attraction and not acting on it.

If you date chaste, one of two things will happen. One is that you will be able to look at this person with a clear mind and say, "You get on my nerves. Goodbye." The other is that, if the relationship is right, something very subtle will begin to develop. There will be a feeling, a realisation that may be almost imperceptible at first, but it will grow steadily until you can look at this person and say, "I love you, and I know it is you. There is not a sexual bond here distorting my emotions. I am thinking clearly, and I know that I love you." Believe me, when that happens, it is better than sex. And it will make sex better when the time is right.

Walter Trobisch once pointed out that when an orchestra tunes up, it doesn't start with the drums and the trumpets. It starts with the flutes and the violins, because otherwise the loud trumpets and drums would drown out the quieter instruments. The same applies to sex and love. Love is very delicate and develops very slowly, but premature sex will drown that love in the intensity of sexual passion.

It is easy to want to give in to sexual feelings. They are often at their strongest when we are with someone we care about. But the old saying is true: "Love takes time." Letting our sexual feelings get the best of us can only hurt love. It pays to wait.

"Can I live chastity even if I am not a virgin?"

Yes, you can! Anyone who comes to understand the beauty and the meaning of sexuality can make a commitment to live chastity, regardless of the past.

The world seems to have a skewed attitude towards sexual activity. People say that once you have started, you are not going to be able to stop. Statistics classify teenagers who have done it only once as "sexually active", even though many of those do not return to sexual activity. Sex education instructors are often told to emphasise abstinence for teens who have not had sexual relationships and contraception for those who have.

Funny, they don't have that attitude about anything else. No one says, "Well, now that you've tried drugs, I guess you'll keep using them. Here's a roach clip – don't burn your fingers." Or, "Well, you got drunk. I guess we'll never see you sober at a party again." People are constantly being urged not to repeat their past mistakes – except when it comes to sex.

A lot of people tend to think that, once they have lost their virginity, they are somehow "tainted" forever. Word might be out among their friends. They feel they have joined a different "club", and there is no going back. Their sex education classes tell them that they had better start looking into contraception. They are uneasy about the Church and wary of God. It becomes easy to drift away from him. It is all so unnecessary. There is hope. You can join literally millions of others across the country and around the world who are returning to lives of chastity after realising that sexual activity was hurting their lives.

If they can do it, you can.

"I want to start over. What steps should I take to ensure I don't mess up again?"

Later in the book, we will talk about some general guidelines for *anyone* who wants to live chastity. Here, however, I want to give some guidelines specifically for those of you who are starting over.

Ask for forgiveness: This goes without saying. The first step to making your life right again is making your relationship with God right again. Go to Confession. There are all kinds of graces attached to the Sacrament of Reconciliation that will make the next steps easier.

Pray: Once you have restored your relationship with God, it is important to continue that relationship. Pray regularly. Attend Mass. Receive communion. Stay close to God. Ask him for the help you will constantly need to live a life of chastity. Along these lines, you should make a special effort to make the Eucharist a part of your life. Jesus said, "Unless you eat the flesh of the Son of man and drink his Blood, you have no life in you" (*Jn* 6:53). How much sexual activity is a result of feeling that we have no life in us? The Eucharist is Jesus – Body, Blood, soul and divinity. It is the whole Jesus, the one who loves you more than anyone, physically present right in front of you. He fills you with his love. There is tremendous supernatural power in the Eucharist.

Try to make the Eucharist a part of your daily life: Receive communion every day. Spend time praying in front of the Blessed Sacrament. Find a church in your area with perpetual adoration (where the Eucharist is displayed in the church or chapel for worship and adoration). If you can't find perpetual adoration, just go to your own church, where he is present in the tabernacle. Spend a half-hour a day, or fifteen minutes a day, or an hour a week, or whatever, in his presence. Pray the Rosary, pray in your own words or just sit there and absorb his love. Ask him to give you his love. Ask him to take charge of your future. Even if it doesn't feel spiritually moving at the time, I guarantee that if you stick with it, this can be a life-changing experience. Over time, it will help you to heal your pain.

Have a buddy system: When you are starting over, or just trying to resist temptation, it is tough to struggle alone. Obviously, you need God's help, which comes through prayer. But it is also good to have a youth leader or a priest or someone who believes what you believe and who is willing to help you to live chastity. You should talk to this person every time you go on a date or even go anywhere with someone you are attracted to. You should tell him or her in advance what your plans are. Being more objective, this person can say, "Hey, you promised you'd never be alone with him (her) in his (her) house again." You should also talk to this person *after* every date, so that you can go over what went right (or wrong). Knowing you are going to do this can be pretty helpful in the heat of temptation. If you slip up again, you will be accountable to someone. That can help you to stop.

Fill your life with positive love: Single people often get involved in sexual activity because they are trying to find the real love that is missing in their lives. Trying to find that love in sex doesn't work. But neither does trying to eliminate sex without dealing with the root of the problem. Humans do not need sex, but we do need love. What should we do when our lives lack love? Sometimes we can't do much about absent parents or problems in our families. We can't help it if the people around us are not very loving. But there is one person you can control – yourself. You can *be* a loving person. That makes a difference. With love, what goes around, comes around. Make an effort to fill your life with love for the people around you. Volunteer some place where people need you – a soup kitchen, a religious education programme, nursing home visitation, whatever. When you spend your time spreading Christ's love, it is amazing how little time you have left to be tempted by counterfeits.

Develop your talents: Unchaste behaviour feeds on low self-esteem. If you don't like yourself, it is more difficult to respect your sexuality. Making mistakes sexually, conversely, causes even lower self-esteem. You can stop that vicious cycle by learning to see your incredible dignity in God's eyes. God put each of us here for a reason. We each have a role to play in his plan. To help us achieve that role, he gave us each gifts. That includes you. You have gifts and talents. Maybe you're good at singing or sports or painting or something else. Whatever you are good at, it's important for you to find those gifts and to develop them. They will give you an outlet for your energy, help you to develop self-discipline and help you to find your own place in God's plan.

Know your limits: If you have been sexually active before, your limits will be different from what they will be for someone who has never had sex. You have probably formed certain habits, and that means you need to be even more vigilant. If being in a certain dark room used to lead to sex, the best thing to do is to avoid that dark room. If certain types of affection used to lead to sex, the best thing to do is to find other forms of affection instead. The old maxim has never been more true: Know thyself. And do not overestimate thine own strength.

MADE FOR LOVE:
The Quest to Find Mr or Mrs Right

"What are some of the characteristics of love?"

I once heard it said that every person has the same two fears: the fear of not being loved and the fear of not being able to give love. I believe that is true. It's not wrong to want to be loved. In fact, we were made that way. We all have a desire to interact with others, to share our lives and to join them to other lives. We all want to feel that there are people around us who genuinely care about us and who will be there for us no matter what. That desire springs from our creation in the image and likeness of God. God is love, and as his creatures, we were created for love.

The problem, however, is that it is sometimes difficult to understand what "love" means. People use the word "love" a lot of different ways. Take me, for instance. I am often heard saying that I love my mum and dad. (Those of you who know them understand why I would say this.) I am also often heard saying that I love pizza. What am I saying when I say I love my mum and dad? I'm saying that I care about them. I'm saying that I love spending time with them and that I talk to them every chance I get. I'm saying that if they needed me, I would do everything humanly possible to help them. I'm saying that I always want what is best for them.

What am I saying when I say I love pizza? Am I saying that I care deeply about pizza? Am I saying that I have a relationship with pizza? Am I saying that if a pizza had a problem, I would be there for the pizza? ("What? Not enough pepperoni? I'll be right there!") Of course not.

When I say I love pizza, I'm just saying that I enjoy eating pizza until I don't want any more pizza. Once I'm tired of the pizza, I don't care what happens to the rest of it. I'll throw it away. I'll feed it to the dog. I'll stick it in the back of the refrigerator until it gets all green and mouldy. It doesn't matter to me anymore. These are two very different definitions of the word "love".

It gets confusing when people start talking about love and especially about loving you. Which way do these people love you? Do they want what is best for you, or do they just want you around because it is good for them, and they don't really care what happens to you? Next time someone looks deeply in your eyes and says, "I love you", look very deeply right back and say, "Would that be pizza love, or the real thing?"

"What does it mean to 'use' someone?"

God created us to live lives of loving interdependence. Because of this "original sin" problem we inherited from Adam and Eve, however, we are not always so good at real love. Instead of looking out for what is best for others, we all have a tendency to want to look out for what is best for ourselves, without caring about the consequences for anyone else.

Using is "pizza love". In using, we treat people the way we would treat a pizza – making them mere "instruments" to satisfy our own desires and not caring what happens to them. No one wants to be loved with "pizza love". We all want to feel that the people in our lives are there because they care about us – because they honestly and sincerely want what is best for us, and they are willing to be there for us and to stick around when times get tough. It hurts to find out that someone who seemed to love you was only using you.

But how often do you use other people? How often do you date someone, not because you want to explore the possibility of spending your lives together, but because this person is good-looking and makes you feel good or makes you more popular? How often do you get friendly with someone, not because you are genuinely interested in this person, but because he has a nice car or a business connection you need? "Pizza love" works both ways. If you want to receive real love, you have to be willing and able to give it. And learning to love – sincerely to want the good of the other – is a life-long process.

How can you tell whether someone loves you or is using you? Ask yourself one simple question: Is this person genuinely interested in what is best for me? Does this person see me as an image and likeness of God and treat me with dignity and respect? Love is not just about dating or romance. It is a daily requirement – we need to live it and to give it in *all* of our relationships – with family, with friends and with everyone we meet in our lives. To fail to love is to miss the entire point of living.

UNDERSTANDING
the other Sex

"Why aren't guys as emotional as women?"

This is a fairly common assumption – that men are not "emotional", that their feelings are not as deep or as intense as women's feelings.

I happen to believe that this assumption is wrong. In both my personal and professional life, I have had the immense privilege of coming to know many very remarkable men and learning from them about the struggles they face – struggles that in many ways are not so different from the struggles I face as a woman.

This question came from a teenager. It is definitely true that teenaged men aren't as visibly "emotional" as teenaged women. (No one is as visibly emotional as teenaged women. I remember once as a teenager crying for an entire day, and nothing was even wrong. It's a hormone thing.) But because men don't show their emotions the way women do, we assume they don't have them. And that is wrong.

Emotions are good. They were created by God to be signposts for our psychological health. Everyone has them. Some people may carry their emotions closer to the surface, while others may have been suppressing their feelings for so long that they are not sure where to find them anymore. But they are in there – always.

The thing is, God made women and men differently. (I'll bet you already knew that.) He not only made us different physically, he made us different emotionally. We tend to live and express our emotions in different ways. Women tend to talk about their feelings – and talk, and talk, and talk. When I am upset, there is nothing more important to me than finding a good friend (or nine good friends – it doesn't matter) and talking the whole thing through, viewing it from several different angles and basically wallowing in the whole situation for a while.

Men, on the other hand, tend to want to be by themselves and think through their problems. They don't tend to share their problems until they are ready to solve them. This behaviour tends to lead to the assumption that relationships don't mean as much to men and they are not as hurt when a relationship ends. I know that is false – I speak to men all the time who are absolutely devastated by the break up of a relationship. In fact, studies show that, on the whole, it takes men far longer to get over relationships than it takes women.

People think that break ups are harder on women because they are often more visibly upset at the end of a relationship. They cry and mourn and talk to their friends for hours on end. But this is exactly why they tend to heal sooner. They get their pain out into the open. They reach out for help. They deal with it. That brings quicker healing.

Men, on the other hand, are more inclined to try to face their pain alone. To compound that tendency, they often face a certain "macho" stereotype in society. They are expected to be "strong and silent". They are not *supposed* to fall apart at the end of a relationship. Combine that expectation with the fact that men are not as verbal as women, and we should not be surprised that men tend to keep more inside. They don't talk as much about their pain or their problems. That, however, is bad. Pain kept inside tends to fester. It gets worse. It is much more difficult to deal with problems that are never aired.

To answer the question: Men *are* emotional. Some men are more emotional than others, just as some women are more emotional than others. But I believe that most men love very deeply and hurt very deeply when they lose love. Because they are wired differently from the way women are, however, they don't express their love or their pain in exactly the same way women do. They may not express that pain. But that doesn't mean it is not there.

I speak as a woman. But I hope I speak for at least some of you men out there. I may not have felt your pain, but I have seen it. I have seen it in your letters and in those of you who come up to me after a talk, sharing with me your devastation over the loss of a love; or your intense love, dedication and concern for a friend, a family member or a woman. I know you guys are out there. And I think you are all very, very wonderful.

Women, don't be so quick to judge men. Just because he isn't talking about it doesn't mean he isn't hurting. And men, remember that admitting you are in pain is not the worst thing that could happen. In fact, talking it out could be among the best things you could do.

"Why is it women seem emotionally unstable at times?"

Here is a male's version of the previous question. Why do the women he sees get so upset sometimes? Why do they cry so much? Why are their emotions always so, well, there, while men are usually so much calmer? There are several reasons for this discrepancy, some of which we have touched upon already. First, especially for teenaged women, there is the hormonal factor. The teenage years are a time of serious hormonal upheaval. The hormonal and reproductive systems are still developing. Hormone levels vacillate wildly. These hormones can play absolute havoc with a woman's emotional state. Women, especially teenaged or pregnant women, often react very emotionally to relatively minor situations or even when there is nothing whatsoever to be upset about. People around them may not like it, and may tell them to "pull themselves together", but that is more easily said than done. Women don't like crying for no reason any more than others like to listen to them.

The second reason, as we discussed above, is that women as a rule express their feelings more than men do. Studies consistently show that women are more verbal than men, speaking up to ten times more words than their male counterparts every day. Therefore, they are more likely to talk about their feelings. Men, as we discussed, seem to be more likely to keep those feelings inside.

Showing or expressing emotion is not in itself a sign of "emotional instability". In fact, identifying and expressing emotion can often be the healthiest thing to do. Feelings are neither bad nor good in themselves. They are signs. Our job is to examine them, to understand where they come from, to control their expression, and to deal with the situation or situations that brought the feelings about.

If someone is feeling and expressing an emotion, it does very little good to say, "Don't feel that way." The feeling is there, and it won't go away just because it is told to do so. The feeling must be examined and dealt with. Feelings need to be taken seriously, but that doesn't give us license to express them any way we choose. This is particularly true when it comes to anger. Angry feelings come from somewhere – frustration, insecurity, maybe even righteous indignation. But taking that anger out on another person is never right. The best thing to do is to work the anger off in some kind of neutral context (running, chopping wood, biting nails in half, whatever) and then deal with the situation and try to figure out where the anger is coming from.

If you are with someone who is sad or crying, the best thing to do is to let that person "let it all out". Crying does help. A friend of mine lost his wife to cancer. He told me, "She used to tell me it was okay to cry – that she felt better after she cried. I always thought, 'That's dumb. After you cry you feel worse.' Now I know she was right. I cry a lot these days."

None of this is to say that a certain individual may or may not be emotionally unstable. Certainly there are enough factors in modern society that could lead to an individual, male or female, being to some extent emotionally unstable. In this case, again, the solution is not just to repress the emotions, but to put the person in contact with a Christian professional who can assist in sorting through the emotions and getting to the root of the problem.

"What do women most want in men?"

We don't want just what you think we want – a good-looking guy with a great body who drives a Porsche. It may sound like a cliché, but most women want a man who loves her and respects her and treasures her; someone who will be trustworthy and who will be a dedicated husband and father. She wants emotional intimacy and companionship and support. She wants someone who is emotionally healthy and who won't flake out when times get tough. She wants someone who loves her in particular, not just women in general. She wants a loving, lifetime spouse.

See? None of that has anything to do with a Porsche.

STARTING & MAINTAINING a Heathy Relationship

"Exactly how far is too far? I've been wondering. Nobody really says. There are lots of steps between kissing and sex."

I particularly love this question and the questions that follow. There are many voices these days encouraging single people to abstain from sex. Unfortunately, very few will go the next step and help us with the nitty-gritty details of what chastity involves.

Many of these questions are questions I myself have asked. Straight answers are sometimes hard to find. I understand, however, the importance of answering these questions well. Remember, I am single too. I strive to live chastity in my dating life. I am not asking you to follow any rules that I am not following myself. But it is important for all of us to understand exactly what chastity entails.

How far can you go and still be chaste? Does chastity mean you have to draw a line down the centre of the room and keep your date on the opposite side? Or does it mean that "anything goes" as long as there is no actual intercourse?

Neither. Chastity is simply about understanding the difference between affection and passion. Affection is good. We experience life through our bodies, so it is only fitting that we have bodily expressions for affection. Hugs, hand holding and kisses can all be ways of expressing loving affection.

We get into trouble, however, when affection becomes passion. You all know what passion is – creating a desire for sexual intercourse or "turning someone on". Is that loving someone? Is that looking out for what is best for that person?

No. It is more like saying, "I love you so much, I am going to make you want something I am not going to give you." That is not loving. It is making it more difficult for that person to resist sexual temptation. It is leading him or her to frustration. This will not help your relationship.

There is nothing wrong with being sexually attracted to each other. That is good. But it is also a challenge – to keep your affection under control and to stop it before it becomes a temptation. When your affection starts leading to a desire to do more, then it is time to cool off – to go biking, or go out for ice cream, or something positive (and public).

What exact behaviours are okay or off limits? We will be discussing those throughout the next several questions.

"Is petting a sin?"

For those of you who don't know what the word "petting" refers to in this context, it means touching, messing with or stimulating the private parts of someone else's body. Those parts were made for sex, and messing with them is a part of sex. Messing with them outside of marriage is a sin in the same way sex outside of marriage is a sin.

I learned this pretty early on in my dating life. But I didn't learn why this kind of behaviour is wrong. After all, you can't get pregnant that way. So what is so bad about it?

First of all, this is not a loving thing to do. Some risks are still present at that level. You are at risk of sexually transmitted infection. A certain level of bonding is definitely occurring. There is even a certain risk of pregnancy if you come into close enough contact. Putting yourself and someone else at that kind of risk is not loving.

Second, as we discussed in the last question, you are creating a desire in someone – a desire you don't intend to fulfil. These parts of the body were designed to create desire for sex. If a couple goes ahead and completes the act of intercourse, that pre-intercourse activity is defined as "foreplay" – what they did to get in the mood for sex. Is it smart to do this when you are not planning to keep going? It would be like going out to your car, starting it, racing the engine for a while, then turning it off and going back inside. It makes very little sense.

Third, you are making it very difficult to stop. You were not made to stop after this kind of activity. It tends to "shut your brain down". I meet very upset people on an extremely regular basis – people who had no intention of going all the way, but who got started in this kind of "affection" and didn't want to stop. (Note: This does not, I repeat, does not mean that if you make a mistake and go this far, you have an excuse to go all the way. If you are not married, you need to muster all of your strength and quit, period.)

Fourth and most important, sex is the language of marriage. At what point does it begin to speak that language? When intercourse occurs? Or before? To answer that question, you have to ask yourself another. If you were married and you found your spouse in bed naked with the next-door neighbour, would you be upset? Chances are, you would. "Oh, honey", your spouse would say. "It's not the way it looks. We're not going to go all the way." Would that make you feel better? I doubt it. Why? Because you would still feel that your marital sexual language had been violated.

There's another question to ask yourself. Think about your future spouse now, still single and out there dating. What don't you want him to do? Do you like the thought of your future wife getting hot and heavy in the backseat with some guy, or of that guy bragging about her in the locker room? Do you like the thought of your future husband in that kind of situation?

Look at your own date. This is somebody's future wife or husband. And your future spouse is probably going on similar dates. "Respect" means treating your dates the way you want your future spouse to be treated right now. If you are involved in sexual activity, even short of intercourse, you are violating your future marriage. You are cheating on your future spouse. You are cheapening the value of the future language of sex in your marriage.

I once talked to a woman who, while she had never "gone all the way" before her marriage, had gone fairly "far" in her dating affection. Her husband told her that she is the only woman he has ever kissed. She said to me, "I wish more than anything in the world I could say the same to him."

She realised something that you will fully realise only after you are married. Sex speaks the language of marriage. And the arousal behaviour leading up to sex speaks the same language. It is a language that, if you marry, you will share exclusively with your spouse. You won't like the thought of your spouse speaking it with someone else or remembering speaking it with someone else.

Sex is the language of marriage. Whatever you have done in the past, I challenge you today to make a decision to respect that language. Sex is a gift – a gift of yourself to your spouse. Don't "parcel it out" piece by piece to your dates over the years.

From now on, save it all – to give when the giving is right.

"Is it wrong to want to have sex before marriage?"

Define "want to have sex". If you mean "have a physical urge to have sex" or "want to give myself totally to someone I am in love with", then it is perfectly normal. Those desires were put there by God as opportunities for us to learn to become loving persons. When you say, "I really want to make love to you, but because it is not what's best for you, I won't", you are being a loving person, and you are growing in chastity. That is good. If by "want to have sex" you mean "decide that we should have sex even though we're not married" or "pressure my boyfriend or girlfriend to do it", then yes, it is wrong. You can't decide what your body will or will not want, but you can decide how you will respond. And deciding to put someone else at risk to satisfy that urge is wrong.

"How can you present your arguments to someone who does not believe the 'ceremony of marriage' is an essential commitment for a lifelong relationship?"

I'm assuming that this person is not a Christian and doesn't believe that God binds people together in marriage or that sex is a renewal of that spiritual bond. What a shame. This person is missing out on a lot.

You can ask, however, why not have the ceremony? If two people really plan to give themselves to each other, and to spend the rest of their lives together, why refuse to say it in public? Why refuse to sign a marriage certificate? Generally, it is because one or the other isn't really sure about staying around forever. If there is no marriage, the back door is always open.

The marriage contract exists to protect the spouses. Joining in a lifelong relationship involves risk for both parties. A woman, in particular, takes a financial risk. She often stops working or works at less than full capacity so she can raise children. The marriage contract guarantees that she and her children will be supported. If her husband leaves her, he legally has to give her a significant percentage of everything he earned while they were married. He has to continue to contribute to her support and to that of the children.

If, however, there is no marriage, there is limited protection. Either person can bail out at any time, no questions asked. Why would someone insist on that kind of arrangement? Makes you wonder, doesn't it?

"I can't stop. Why is it so difficult to live chastity sometimes? I know it's the right thing to do, but sometimes it's a real struggle anyway."

We all see some kind of gap between conviction and action somewhere in our lives, whether in eating, exercise, prayer or whatever. We know what we should do, but we don't always do it. The good news is that we are in good company. In his letter to the Romans, St Paul said, "I do not understand my own actions. For I do not do what I want, but I do the very thing I hate" (*Rom* 7:15). So, if a guy as holy as St Paul had to deal with this problem, it must be universal.

What is the problem? As St Paul goes on to say, "Now if I do what I do not want … it is no longer I that do it, but sin which dwells within me" (*Rom* 7:16-17). This is because we are all affected by original sin – we are inclined to do things we know are not good for us. There is a constant battle between good and evil going on inside of us.

So what is the answer? "Oh, well, sin lives in me, so I guess I can't fight it. I'll use a condom and everything will be fine." Wrong. Especially with a gift as beautiful as sexuality, we are called to struggle against our sinful nature, to live up to our dignity. When it comes to sex, this can be difficult.

First of all, the human sexual urge is very strong. Once we get tempted, we are really tempted. There is a reason for that. Our bodies are made to move forward, towards intercourse. If they were not made that way, people would be satisfied just making out all the time, and the world would never be repopulated. But once you get the engine rolling, it is a lot more difficult to stop. Your brain shuts off. So anyone who tries to be chaste, but doesn't avoid those tempting situations is going to have a problem. This is especially true for people who have done it and are trying to start over. Habits are formed, and it is very easy for one thing to lead to another when that is where they have always gone before.

There are deeper reasons for repeated failure of sexual self-control. We have talked about how many unmarried people are involved in sexual activity because they are looking for love. The ones who have experienced the least love in their lives are the ones who are most likely to be involved in sexual activity, and they are the ones who have the most difficult time quitting. And it is no wonder. If you are one of these people, and you try to quit without dealing with the lack of love in your life, you will still be tempted (often subconsciously) to seek counterfeit love in sexual activity. You are trying to fill a void that still exists in your life – a void sex cannot fill. But that void makes the temptation much more powerful. You need to fill that void – with real love.

No matter how hard you try to live chastity, you are almost bound for failure if you don't base your efforts on prayer. The tendency towards sin in us is very strong, and we need God's grace and his help if we are going to succeed. Chastity is like a muscle. When you first lift a weight, it can feel very heavy. But the stronger the muscle gets, the easier it is to lift the weight. And if the Holy Spirit is behind you holding the bar, lifting the weight is a whole lot easier. That strength comes through prayer.

"I really want to live chastity. I've tried to stop having sex, but I must be too weak or something. I just keep going back. I'm starting to feel really bad about myself."

You may be unsuccessful at living chastity because you are not fuelling your efforts with a lot of prayer. Maybe you are failing because you are not avoiding tempting situations. Or maybe you are subconsciously looking for love.

"How do you rekindle relationships that have been destroyed by sexual activity?"

The first question to ask is not "How?" but "Should I?" The first step is to stop sexual activity. Completely. Sex creates a strong bond that distorts your true feelings for each other. You need to cease all sexually arousing affection before you can determine how you feel about each other or repair any damage sexual activity has done to your relationship.

Stopping sexual activity is much easier said than done. We have talked about some of the difficulties for an individual in starting over. A couple who have had sex will have a far more difficult time stopping while remaining together. I am not saying that it can't be done – just that you need to be very vigilant. Habits have formed, and you need to be extremely aware of them so that you can avoid tempting situations. After you have abstained for a while, see how things go. Are you able to restrain yourselves sexually out of love for each other? Are you getting along better? Do you recognise now that your sexual activity was hurting you and your relationship?

If the answer is yes, and you've been able to work through your problems, then move forward cautiously. You may have accomplished something very significant, but you still need plenty of time to be certain. If the answer is no – if you haven't been able to work out your problems, or if you keep falling back into sexual sin – then it is time to end the relationship. Don't drag your feet once you realise this. Sticking around in a damaged relationship will only make things worse.

Chastity Guidelines

Here are several suggestions to help you live chastity.

Know your limits: You need to decide in advance what is acceptable and what is unacceptable behaviour. That does not mean, "Well, taking our clothes off is okay, but not intercourse." It means knowing what situations will tempt you to sexual behaviour and avoiding them. If, for example, being in a dark room alone used to lead to sexual intercourse and being there makes you want to do it again, you should probably avoid dark rooms.

Likewise, you need to know and believe that unchaste behaviour is bad. Then you need to act accordingly. When someone "puts a move on you", you need to intercept it. Immediately. It is easy when you are in that situation to think, "He's just doing this because he loves me." Maybe he loves you, but what he is doing is not loving behaviour. It is exploitative.

You need to make a decision: "Touch me there, and I go home." And then follow through. If he doesn't listen the next time, you should say, "Touch me there again, and I go home for good." The same goes for someone who is pressuring you or trying to seduce you. There is no reason to hang around.

Be selective about dating: Dating is probably the single most overrated activity in the history of the universe. On TV, single people date constantly and we feel like something is wrong with us if we don't date that often too. Puhleeease! If there is no one around that you want to date, what is the point? If a person isn't going to respect your sexuality and your limits, what is the point? You don't need to date just for the sake of dating. In the end, the most important relationships in your life are going to be your friendships, both male and female. And you will have a lot more fun with friends than you will have dating someone you don't like or who doesn't respect you. Save dates for special people whom you respect and who respect you.

Be sure there is plenty of real love in your life: Maintaining strong, loving relationships with your family and friends is without a doubt one of the best ways to maintain chastity. As we have seen, much of today's sexual activity is fuelled by a hunger for love. If your "tank" is full, you won't be as tempted to look for counterfeit love in sexual relationships.

Learn about chastity: I know that after reading this book you might feel that you have learned all there is to know about the subject. But guess what? There is more. Keep reading. The more you understand, the stronger you will be.

Stay close to God: Chastity is difficult in this day and age. If you try to live chastily without God, I absolutely guarantee that you will fail. His grace provides the fuel you need to resist the temptations that will come your way on a daily basis. Pray daily for chastity. Pray for an understanding of it. Pray for the strength to live it.

FINDING
Mr or Mrs Right

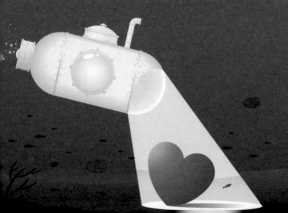

"How do you know you've met the love of your life?"

In the movies, people know exactly when they are in love. They look into each other's eyes, and time stands still. The music begins to play, and *boom*, they are in love. As soon as they hear that music, they know it must be time to fall in love.

Unfortunately, real life doesn't work that way. Our lives don't have soundtracks, and it takes a lot more than a couple of verses of a song for real love to develop. Being "in love" does not mean "I get a warm, wonderful feeling around you" or "I am very sexually attracted to you". It means, "I want to share the rest of my life with you. I want to have children with you. I want to grow old with you. I want to marry you." Sexual attraction and wonderful feelings are a part of that, but they are not the whole story.

"In love" is more than just a feeling. It is also a decision. This is important, so I am going to repeat it: *"In love" is not just a feeling. It is a decision.* The love of your life is, or should be, the person you marry. This is obviously a very important decision, and it should not be based simply on how you "feel". Feelings can come and go for a lot of different reasons, ranging from your emotional state to your choice of breakfast food. Your feelings alone don't know how to make good long-term decisions. They need the help and co-operation of your brain.

I think a lot of people spend a lot of time trying to "define" their feelings – trying to decide if they are "in love" or just "in like" or whatever. Unless you are considering marrying someone, this is a waste of time. "In love" is a decision. It is a part of the marriage decision. Until you are making that kind of decision, don't worry about naming your relationships. Just enjoy them.

"How do you know when a guy really loves you?"

You will know he loves you by the way he treats you. Is his primary concern what is best for you? Does he look out for you? Is he considerate of your feelings? Does he allow you the freedom to do what you feel you need to do? Does he encourage you to keep up with your other friends and interests, even if that may mean spending less time with him? As I said before, one of the most important considerations is how he treats you sexually. Does he respect you? Does he make an effort to avoid tempting situations and to keep his desires under control so that he won't do anything that could hurt you? Does he protect your reputation?

If you find someone like this, you have found a treasure. Of course, you shouldn't marry a person just because he has these qualities, but you should never marry someone who does not have them.

"How will I know when I've met the person I should marry?"

The choice of a spouse should not be based on "I get a warm, wonderful feeling whenever we're together, and I want to have that warm, wonderful feeling forever so let's get married." Feelings, as we have discussed, have no logic of their own. They need to be acknowledged, of course, but they need considerable assistance from your brain.

Marriage means choosing the person you will spend the rest of your life with. This, as you may have guessed, is a very long time to spend with one person. This person will live with you, eat meals with you, sleep with you and go on holiday with you. More important yet, this person will share your children. You need to choose wisely. The decision should not be made based on feelings alone. You need to ask yourself some tough questions. The decision has to be based on solid considerations.

Will this person be a good spouse? Is she mature enough to put her own selfish desires aside to look out for what is best for the family? Is he prepared to be a good provider? What is his track record? Is he responsible enough to get a good job and keep it? Will this person be a good parent? Can you stand the thought of your children turning out *exactly* like this person?

They will, you know. Children spend a lot of time with their parents and consequently pick up many or most of their parents' character traits. You had better like your spouse's traits a *lot*, because you will be seeing them again in your children.

If something were to happen to you, would you completely trust this person, *alone*, with the task of raising and forming your children? This is not a pleasant thought, but it is an important consideration. Not everyone dies at a ripe old age with great-grandchildren gathered around the bed. Sometimes a parent dies and leaves young children in the care of the other parent. If you feel that you would need to be around to correct or lessen this person's influence on your children, you are considering the wrong person.

Does this person share your faith in God? God does not give us children so that we can mould them into the coolest, most popular people in school. Our job is to get them to heaven. To do that, we need to raise them believing in God and in his Church. It's tough to do that when only one parent believes. Saying, "This is right and this is wrong, and I want you to ignore Mummy until you are thirty-five", does not work. Small children ask about eighty skillion questions in a single day. The answers to those questions go a long way towards forming the kind of adults they will become. Who will be answering those questions for your children?

Does this person you are marrying have sexual self-control? Single people sometimes have this idea that marriage is just some kind of lifelong sex festival and that as long as they have each other, they will never be tempted by other people. Wrong. There are times in every marriage when one spouse or the other is sexually unavailable due to illness, the last months of pregnancy, or travel. There are also times when spouses just get on each other's nerves. At times like this, other people can seem very appealing. That can be dangerous, because there are plenty of very attractive people out there who are willing to make themselves available to married men and women. Do you want to marry someone who has never said no to sex? If he is not good at saying no at eighteen, it won't be any different at forty. Do you want to worry about whether or not your spouse is being faithful? What kind of marriage can you have with someone you couldn't trust on a business trip?

These are very important questions, and if you are not comfortable with all of the answers, you should definitely not marry this person. None of this is to say that feelings play no role at all in a marriage decision. You don't have to say, "Well, I suppose you would make a good spouse and parent, so even though I don't particularly like you, I guess I'll marry you." You need to be happy and excited about the prospect of spending your life with someone. Your brain, however, must also acknowledge this person as a good catch.

Don't listen to your heart alone or your head alone. Wait until your heart and your head agree.

"What is the difference between love and infatuation?"

Love loves the other exactly as he is. Infatuation loves the image he has built of the other person.

Love is being in love with *someone*. Infatuation is being "in love with love". Love happens gradually, over time. Infatuation happens quickly.

In love, two people get along *better as* time goes by. In infatuation, fights become more frequent and more severe over time.

In love, friends and family tend to approve. In infatuation, friends and family often disapprove. Love sees the other as an important part of his world. Infatuation sees the other as his whole world. Love brings out the best in you. It makes you more organised, more productive and more effective. Infatuation can bring out the worst in you. It can make you less organised, less productive and less your "real" self.

Love is consistent. Infatuation comes and goes. Love seeks to give. Infatuation seeks to get.[1]

"Doesn't sex go downhill once a couple gets married?"

This is one of the most common and most ridiculous myths I've ever heard. In fact, there have been a lot of polls done on sexual activity. Everyone loves to do polls about sex.

[1.] Adapted from Ray Short, *Sex, Love or Infatuation* (Minneapolis: Augsburg Publishing House, 1990).

Who's having sex? Who's having sex the most frequently? Who's having the most satisfying sex? Interestingly enough, they have done several of these polls over the last twenty-five years or so. I don't know why they bother. All the polls reach the same conclusion. The most sexually satisfied people – the people who are having the most frequent, most fulfilling sex – are married people. Not just any married people, but *highly religious married people who have saved sex for marriage.*

Why would this be? Is it about technique? Are married people "better" at sex? Not necessarily. This has nothing to do with technique. It has to do with *context*. Sex has an inherent meaning. It means "forever". Committed married people *mean* forever. They understand what they are saying in sexual expression, and they are saying it honestly. And they know that the other is saying it honestly. They are truly "giving themselves" in their sexual union. Married people also have nothing to fear. They don't have to fear pregnancy and single parenthood, because they are committed to staying together. They don't have to fear sexually transmitted infections, because if they are both disease-free and faithful, there are no diseases to transmit. They don't have to fear being used and abandoned, because if they believe in their marriage vows, neither one will abandon the other.

Why do many of the studies mention that married couples who have saved sex for marriage have more satisfying sex lives? Simple. In the first place, people who save sex for marriage are people who understand the meaning of sex. They recognise the level of commitment it signifies and requires, and they abstained during their dating years (which isn't always easy!) out of respect for that language and out of love for a spouse they may not even have known yet. Someone who can do that is someone who has gained a significant degree of self-control, someone who knows what sex says and someone who can be trusted to be faithful. With a spouse like that, it is much easier to give a complete gift of self, knowing that the other can be trusted with the gift.

Second, a couple who wait for marriage learn about sex together, from each other. They have no one to compare the other to, no memories of other people to hinder their enjoyment of each other. No one likes the thought of being compared to another lover, and for a virgin bride and groom, no comparisons can be made. (*Note:* I am not saying that people who have made sexual mistakes in the past cannot have a happy, satisfying marital sex life.)

Epilogue

Chastity is not just the answer to the question: "How do I avoid AIDS, or pregnancy, or sexually transmitted infections?" Chastity also helps us to answer the deeper questions: "Who am I?" "Who is God in my life?" "How do I find love?"

Whether you are a student at university, a single adult or a teenager, I hope that some of what you have found in these pages applies to your own life. And I pray that, as a result of what you have read here, you have made a commitment, or a recommitment, to living a life of real love – chastity.

We talked in the beginning of the book about how the Church doesn't make us do anything. We have free will, and our free decisions determine the course of our lives. But make no mistake. Making a commitment to living chastity is not optional for the Christian. Deciding to respect our sexuality is a part of the decision to follow Jesus Christ. Christ never said, "Some of my followers keep my commandments, and some of my followers don't." He said, "If you love me, you will keep my commandments" (Jn 14:15). He knew we would stumble and fall sometimes. He knew he was asking us to follow a "narrow road". He expects us, however, to try. When we fall, he expects us to repent, to get back up, to brush ourselves off and to start trying all over again.

Chastity does not come automatically. As a result of original sin, we are inclined to do things we should not do. Our hearts are not totally corrupt, but neither are they completely pure. As St John Paul II said, the human heart is a "battlefield" between love and lust. Each is constantly trying to gain the upper hand. The strength to live chastity does not, I repeat, does not come from us. It is a gift from God – a gift available to anyone who asks it of him. Anyone who commits to a life of chastity, but doesn't pray for the strength to live it is setting himself up for failure. Chastity does get easier over time. It is, as I said before, like a muscle. When you first start lifting weights, it seems very difficult. But as you continue to work out, over weeks and months, the same amount of weight becomes easier to lift. The load is still just as heavy, but you have developed the muscle you need to handle it. And prayer is like having the Holy Spirit behind you with his finger under the barbell, helping you to lift.

Likewise, every time you encounter a tempting situation and you call on the Holy Spirit and you successfully resist, you become a little bit stronger, a little more chaste. You develop a little bit more spiritual "muscle".

Please don't ever take chastity for granted. Don't ever start to think you have developed enough muscle or that you no longer need the Holy Spirit behind you, helping you to lift that weight. You do. Without the Holy Spirit, that barbell would come crashing in on your head, no matter how strong you think you are. Don't ever think you have attained perfect chastity. You have not. I have not. There is no such thing in this life. You are still running around in a human body, and that body is still programmed to respond in certain ways to certain stimuli. It is when you take your guard down, when you stop praying because you think you have it all figured out, that you are in the most danger. Christ, in speaking to his disciples, said, "If you keep my commandments, you will abide in my love, just as I have kept my Father's commandments and abide in his love. These things I have spoken to you, that my joy may be in you, and that your joy may be full" (*Jn* 15:10-11).

That, in a nutshell, is why I do what I do. I don't give these talks just because I want to help you avoid AIDS, unmarried pregnancy and sexually transmitted infections. It's true that I don't want to see you go through any of those traumas. But I want more for you than just that. I want you to experience joy – the authentic love and joy that Christ was talking about, the joy that comes from following all of his commandments and living our lives according to his instruction manual.

You can't find that joy in "safe sex". You probably won't find it in mere "abstinence" practised out of fear. But you will begin to find that joy and that peace in living lives of real, authentic chastity.

Don't just abstain. Be radical. Be chaste.

The Catholic Survival Guide to Dating & Relationships For Teens

Mary Beth Bonacci

Whether single or currently in a relationship, this frank and honest guide will give Catholic teenagers the wisdom to choose wisely when journeying along the perplexing road of dating and relationships.

PA 27   ISBN 978 1 78469 132 5